Walking in the Word

SCRIPTURE MEMORY VERSE PRO

Gospel Light is an evangelical Christian publisher dedicated to serving the local church. We believe God's vision for Gospel Light is to provide church leaders with biblical, user-friendly materials that will help them evangelize, disciple and minister to children, youth and families.

It is our prayer that this Gospel Light resource will help you discover biblical truth for your own life and help you minister to others. May God richly bless you.

For a free catalog of resources from Gospel Light, please contact your Christian supplier or contact us at 1-800-4-GOSPEL *or* www.gospellight.com.

PUBLISHING STAFF
William T. Greig, Publisher
Dr. Elmer L. Towns, Senior Consulting Publisher
Pam Weston, Senior Editor
Patti Pennington Virtue, Associate Editor
Jeff Kempton, Editorial Assistant
Hilary Young, Editorial Assistant
Kyle Duncan, Associate Publisher
Bayard Taylor, M.Div., Senior Editor, Biblical and Theological Issues
Dr. Gary S. Greig, Senior Advisor, Biblical and Theological Issues
Samantha Hsu, Designer

ISBN 0-8307-2899-6
© 2001 First Place
All rights reserved.
Printed in the U.S.A.

All Scripture quotations are taken from the *Holy Bible, New International Version*®. Copyright © 1973, 1978, 1984 by International Bible Society. Used by permission of Zondervan Publishing House. All rights reserved.

THE VALUE OF SCRIPTURE MEMORY

I have hidden your word in my heart that I might not sin against you.
Psalm 119:11

Scripture memory is an important part of the Christian life. Three reasons to memorize Scripture:

- **To handle difficult situations**—A heartfelt knowledge of God's Word equips us to handle any situation that we might face.

- **To overcome temptation**—Knowledge of Scripture and the strength that comes with the ability to use it are important parts of putting on the full armor of God in preparation for spiritual warfare (see Ephesians 6:10-18).

- **To get guidance**—Learning to hide God's Word in your heart will allow His light to direct your decisions and actions throughout your day.

Anyone can memorize Scripture. However, it does take a commitment of time and a willing heart. To memorize Scripture you must have a positive attitude and say with Paul, "I can do everything through him who gives me strength" (Philippians 4:13).

This handy little book of Scripture verses can go everywhere with you. Also available are First Place Scripture memory CDs and audiocassettes with these same verses set to inspirational music to provide an additional aid to take the verses with you as you drive, work or exercise.

Through a lifestyle that includes memorizing Scripture, the Holy Spirit will be able to bring the truth to your mind in difficult times, when temptation comes or when seeking guidance for your life. God's Spirit will also bring you opportunities to share Scripture with others as you witness to them, as well as times when you need to encourage others. Remember, as you hide God's Word in your heart, you will truly be storing up treasures from heaven!

Giving Christ First Place

But seek first his kingdom and his righteousness,
and all these things will be given to you as well.

week one

Matthew 6:33

Giving Christ First Place

week one

Matthew 6:33

Giving Christ First Place

If you believe, you will receive
whatever you ask for in prayer.

week two

Matthew 21:22

GIVING CHRIST FIRST PLACE

week two

MATTHEW 21:22

Giving Christ First Place

Whoever has my commands and obeys them,
he is the one who loves me.
He who loves me will be loved by my Father,
and I too will love him and show myself to him.

week three

John 14:21

Giving Christ First Place

week three

John 14:21

Giving Christ First Place

You know my folly, O God;
my guilt is not hidden from you.

week four

Psalm 69:5

Giving Christ First Place

week four

Psalm 69:5

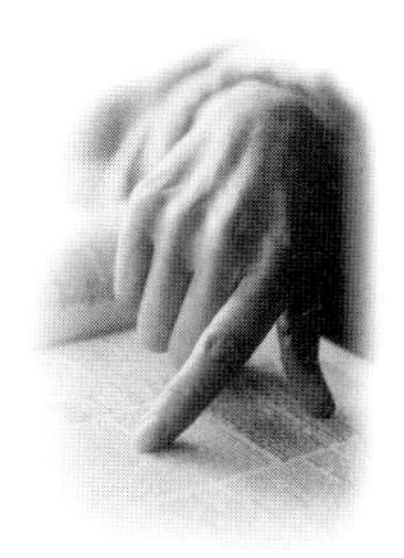

Giving Christ First Place

No temptation has seized you except what is common to man. And God is faithful; he will not let you be tempted beyond what you can bear. But when you are tempted, he will also provide a way out so that you can stand up under it.

week five

1 Corinthians 10:13

Giving Christ First Place

week five

1 CORINTHIANS 10:13

GIVING CHRIST FIRST PLACE

Man does not live on bread alone,
but on every word that comes from the mouth of God.

week six

MATTHEW 4:4

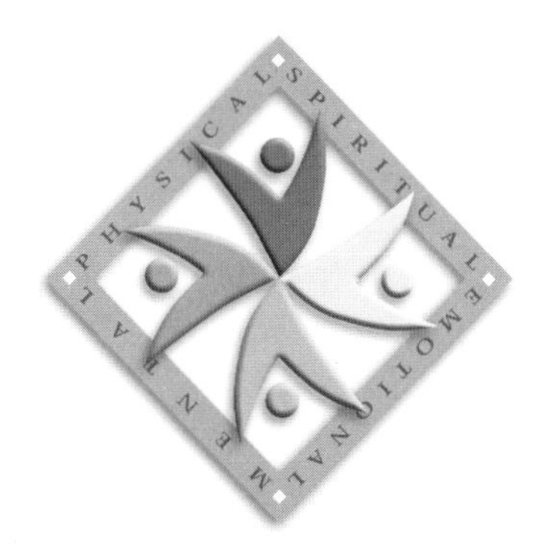

Giving Christ First Place

week six

Matthew 4:4

Giving Christ First Place

Do not conform any longer to the pattern of this world,
but be transformed by the renewing of your mind.
Then you will be able to test and approve what God's
will is—his good, pleasing and perfect will.

week seven

Romans 12:2

Giving Christ First Place

week seven

Romans 12:2

GIVING CHRIST FIRST PLACE

Do you not know that your body is a temple of the Holy Spirit, who is in you, whom you have received from God? You are not your own; you were bought at a price. Therefore honor God with your body.

week eight

1 CORINTHIANS 6:19,20

GIVING CHRIST FIRST PLACE

week eight

1 CORINTHIANS 6:19,20

Commit to the LORD whatever you do,
and your plans will succeed.

week nine

PROVERBS 16:3

GIVING CHRIST FIRST PLACE

week nine

PROVERBS 16:3

GIVING CHRIST FIRST PLACE

A new command I give you: Love one another. As I have loved you, so you must love one another. By this all men will know that you are my disciples, if you love one another.

week ten

JOHN 13:34,35

GIVING CHRIST FIRST PLACE

week ten

JOHN 13:34,35

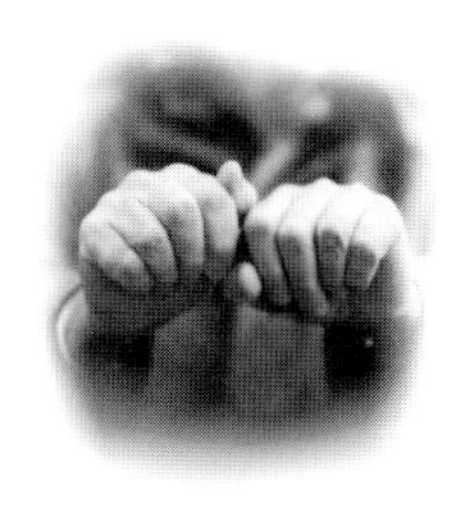

Everyday Victory for Everyday People

Now what I am commanding you today is not too difficult for you or beyond your reach.

week one

Deuteronomy 30:11

Everyday Victory for Everyday People

week one

Deuteronomy 30:11

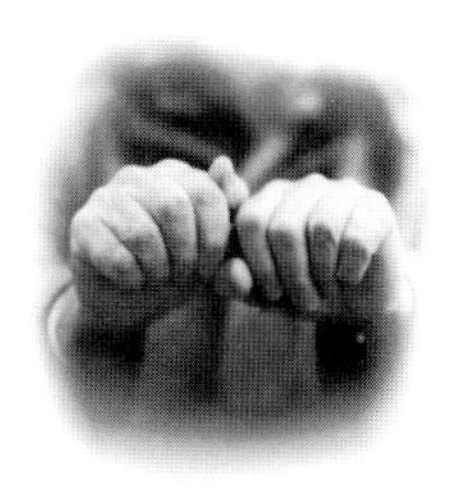

Everyday Victory for Everyday People

It is better not to vow than to make a vow and not fulfill it.

week two

Ecclesiastes 5:5

Everyday Victory for Everyday People

week two

Ecclesiastes 5:5

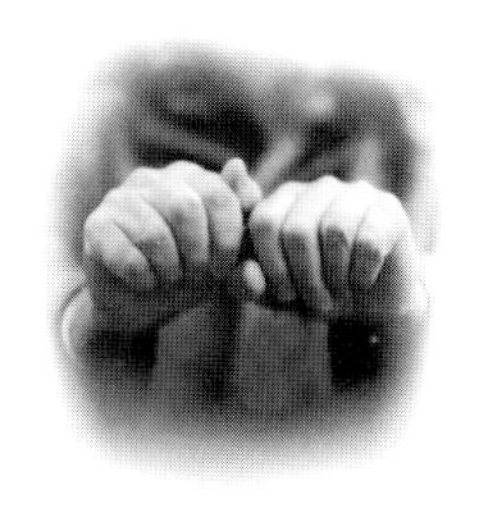

Everyday Victory for Everyday People

Be self-controlled and alert. Your enemy the devil prowls around like a roaring lion looking for someone to devour.

week three

1 Peter 5:8

Everyday Victory for Everyday People

week three

1 Peter 5:8

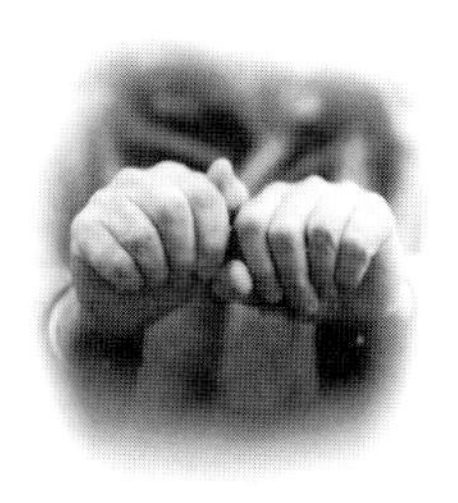

EVERYDAY VICTORY FOR EVERYDAY PEOPLE

The weapons we fight with are not the weapons of the world. On the contrary, they have divine power to demolish strongholds.

week four

2 CORINTHIANS 10:4

Everyday Victory for Everyday People

week four

2 CORINTHIANS 10:4

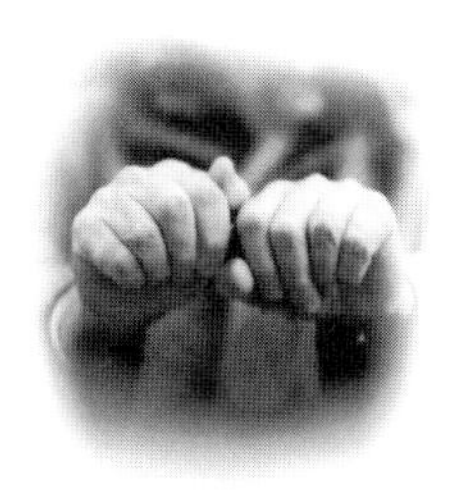

Everyday Victory for Everyday People

Call to me and I will answer you and tell you great and unsearchable things you do not know.

week five

Jeremiah 33:3

EVERYDAY VICTORY FOR EVERYDAY PEOPLE

week five

JEREMIAH 33:3

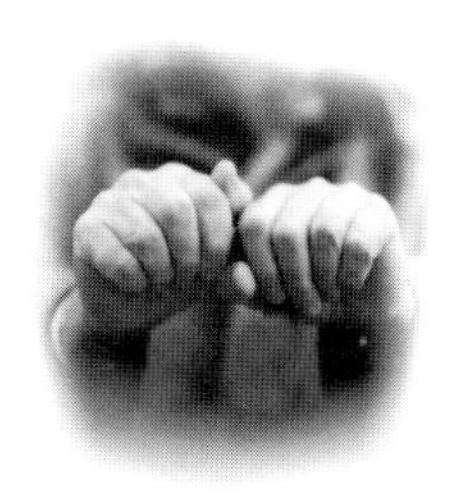

Everyday Victory for Everyday People

We make it our goal to please him, whether we are at home in the body or away from it.

week six

2 Corinthians 5:9

Everyday Victory for Everyday People

week six

2 CORINTHIANS 5:9

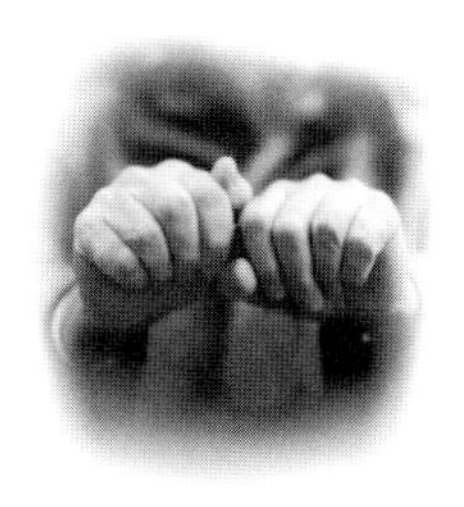

Everyday Victory for Everyday People

However, I consider my life worth nothing to me, if only I may finish the race and complete the task the Lord Jesus has given me—the task of testifying to the gospel of God's grace.

week seven

Acts 20:24

Everyday Victory for Everyday People

week seven

Acts 20:24

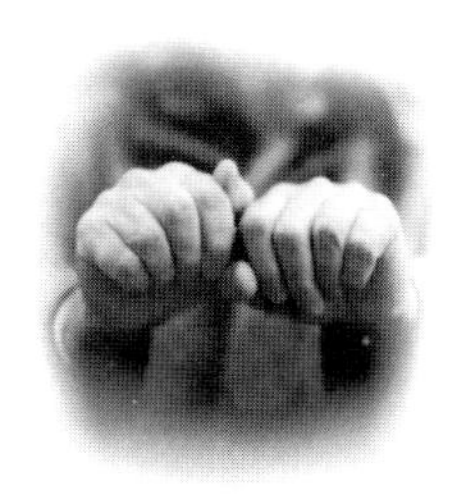

Everyday Victory for Everyday People

"Not by might nor by power, but by my Spirit," says the Lord Almighty.

week eight

Zechariah 4:6

Everyday Victory for Everyday People

week eight

Zechariah 4:6

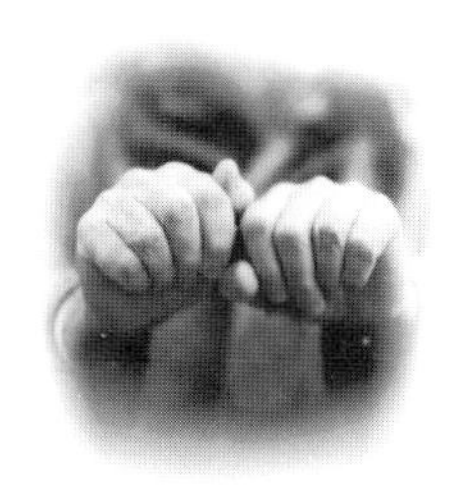

Everyday Victory for Everyday People

Therefore, there is now no condemnation for those who are in Christ Jesus.

week nine

Romans 8:1

Everyday Victory for Everyday People

week nine

Romans 8:1

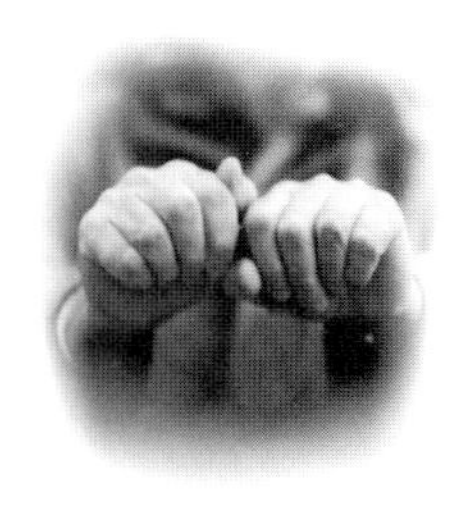

EVERYDAY VICTORY FOR EVERYDAY PEOPLE

Those who know your name will trust in you,
for you, LORD, have never forsaken those who seek you.

week ten

PSALM 9:10

Everyday Victory for Everyday People

week ten

Psalm 9:10

Life Under Control

Restore to me the joy of your salvation and grant me a willing spirit, to sustain me.

week one

Psalm 51:12

Life Under Control

week one

Psalm 51:12

Life Under Control

May the God of hope fill you with all joy and peace as you trust in him, so that you may overflow with hope by the power of the Holy Spirit.

week two

Romans 15:13

LIFE UNDER CONTROL

week two

ROMANS 15:13

Life Under Control

Finally, brothers, whatever is true, whatever is noble, whatever is right, whatever is pure, whatever is lovely, whatever is admirable—if anything is excellent or praiseworthy—think about such things.

week three

Philippians 4:8

Life Under Control

week three

Philippians 4:8

Life Under Control

I have been crucified with Christ and I no longer live, but Christ lives in me. The life I live in the body, I live by faith in the Son of God, who loved me and gave himself for me.

week four

Galatians 2:20

LIFE UNDER CONTROL

week four

GALATIANS 2:20

Life Under Control

I have learned the secret of being content in any and every situation, whether well fed or hungry, whether living in plenty or in want. I can do everything through him who gives me strength.

week five

Philippians 4:12,13

LIFE UNDER CONTROL

week five

PHILIPPIANS 4:12,13

Life Under Control

Do not think of yourself more highly than you ought, but rather think of yourself with sober judgment, in accordance with the measure of faith God has given you.

week six

Romans 12:3

Life Under Control

week six

Romans 12:3

LIFE UNDER CONTROL

If anyone considers himself religious and yet does not keep a tight rein on his tongue, he deceives himself and his religion is worthless.

week seven

JAMES 1:26

Life Under Control

week seven

James 1:26

Life Under Control

If anyone would come after me, he must deny himself and take up his cross daily and follow me.

week eight

Luke 9:23

LIFE UNDER CONTROL

week eight

LUKE 9:23

LIFE UNDER CONTROL

Let us consider how we may spur one another on toward love and good deeds. Let us not give up meeting together, as some are in the habit of doing, but let us encourage one another—and all the more as you see the Day approaching.

week nine

HEBREWS 10:24,25

Life Under Control

week nine

Hebrews 10:24,25

Life Under Control

May God himself, the God of peace, sanctify you through and through. May your whole spirit, soul and body be kept blameless at the coming of our Lord Jesus Christ.

week ten

1 Thessalonians 5:23

Life Under Control

week ten

1 Thessalonians 5:23

Life That Wins

But God demonstrates his own love for us in this: While we were still sinners, Christ died for us.

week one

Romans 5:8

LIFE THAT WINS

week one

ROMANS 5:8

LIFE THAT WINS

"For I know the plans I have for you," declares the LORD,
"plans to prosper you and not to harm you,
plans to give you hope and a future."

week two

JEREMIAH 29:11

LIFE THAT WINS

week two

JEREMIAH 29:11

Life That Wins

And without faith it is impossible to please God, because anyone who comes to him must believe that he exists and that he rewards those who earnestly seek him.

week three

HEBREWS 11:6

Life That Wins

week three

Hebrews 11:16

Life That Wins

The fruit of the Spirit is love, joy, peace, patience, kindness, goodness, faithfulness, gentleness and self-control.

week four

Galatians 5:22,23

Life That Wins

week four

Galatians 5:22,23

LIFE THAT WINS

Do not grieve, for the joy of the LORD is your strength.

week five

NEHEMIAH 8:10

LIFE THAT WINS

week five

NEHEMIAH 8:10

Life That Wins

And the peace of God, which transcends all understanding, will guard your hearts and your minds in Christ Jesus.

week six

Philippians 4:7

Life That Wins

week six

Philippians 4:7

Life That Wins

Let us not become weary in doing good, for at the proper time we will reap a harvest if we do not give up.

week seven

Galatians 6:9

LIFE THAT WINS

week seven

GALATIANS 6:9

Life That Wins

Therefore, as God's chosen people, holy and dearly loved, clothe yourselves with compassion, kindness, humility, gentleness and patience.

week eight

Colossians 3:12

LIFE THAT WINS

week eight

COLOSSIANS 3:12

LIFE THAT WINS

Take my yoke upon you and learn from me, for I am gentle and humble in heart, and you will find rest for your souls.

week nine

MATTHEW 11:29

Life That Wins

week nine

Matthew 11:29

Life That Wins

So I say, live by the Spirit, and you will not gratify the desires of the sinful nature.

week ten

Galatians 5:16

Life That Wins

week ten

Galatians 5:16

Seeking God's Best

Then Jesus declared, "I am the bread of life.
He who comes to me will never go hungry,
and he who believes in me will never be thirsty."

week one

John 6:35

Seeking God's Best

week one

John 6:35

Seeking God's Best

"Ever since the time of your forefathers you have turned away from my decrees and have not kept them. Return to me, and I will return to you," says the LORD Almighty.

week two

Malachi 3:7

Seeking God's Best

week two

Malachi 3:7

SEEKING GOD'S BEST

Give thanks in all circumstances,
for this is God's will for you in Christ Jesus.

week three

1 THESSALONIANS 5:18

SEEKING GOD'S BEST

week three

1 THESSALONIANS 5:18

SEEKING GOD'S BEST

While we wait for the blessed hope—the glorious appearing of our great God and Savior, Jesus Christ, who gave himself for us to redeem us from all wickedness and to purify for himself a people that are his very own, eager to do what is good.

week four

TITUS 2:13,14

SEEKING GOD'S BEST

week four

TITUS 2:13,14

Seeking God's Best

The Lord does not look at the things man looks at.
Man looks at the outward appearance,
but the Lord looks at the heart.

week five

1 Samuel 16:7

SEEKING GOD'S BEST

week five

1 SAMUEL 16:7

Seeking God's Best

Submit yourselves, then, to God.
Resist the devil, and he will flee from you.

week six

James 4:7

Seeking God's Best

week six

James 4:7

Seeking God's Best

My God will meet all your needs
according to his glorious riches in Christ Jesus.

week seven

Philippians 4:19

SEEKING GOD'S BEST

week seven

PHILIPPIANS 4:19

Seeking God's Best

Joshua told the people, "Consecrate yourselves, for tomorrow the LORD will do amazing things among you."

week eight

Joshua 3:5

Seeking God's Best

week eight

Joshua 3:5

SEEKING GOD'S BEST

My dear brothers, stand firm. Let nothing move you.
Always give yourselves fully to the work of the Lord,
because you know that your labor in the Lord is not in vain.

week nine

1 CORINTHIANS 15:58

SEEKING GOD'S BEST

week nine

1 CORINTHIANS 15:58

Seeking God's Best

You prepare a table before me in the presence of my enemies.
You anoint my head with oil; my cup overflows.
Surely goodness and love will follow me all the days of my life,
and I will dwell in the house of the LORD forever.

week ten

Psalm 23:5,6

Seeking God's Best

week ten

Psalm 23:5,6

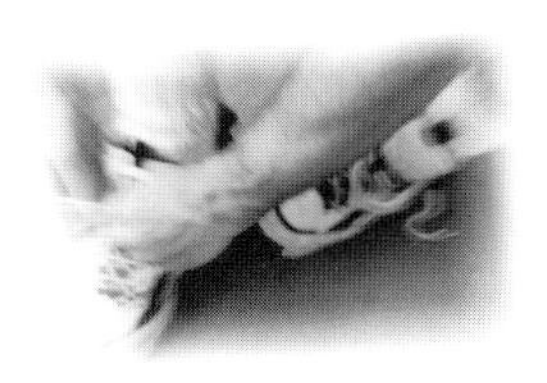

Pressing On to the Prize

I press on toward the goal to win the prize
for which God has called me heavenward in Christ Jesus.

week one

Philippians 3:14

PRESSING ON TO THE PRIZE

week one

PHILIPPIANS 3:14

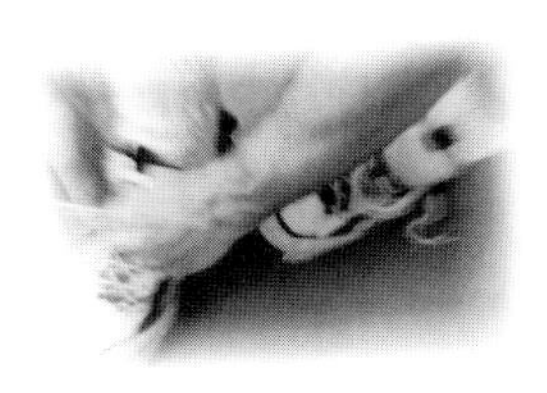

Pressing On to the Prize

By faith Abraham, when called to go to a place
he would later receive as his inheritance, obeyed and went,
even though he did not know where he was going.

week two

Hebrews 11:8

Pressing On to the Prize

week two

Hebrews 11:8

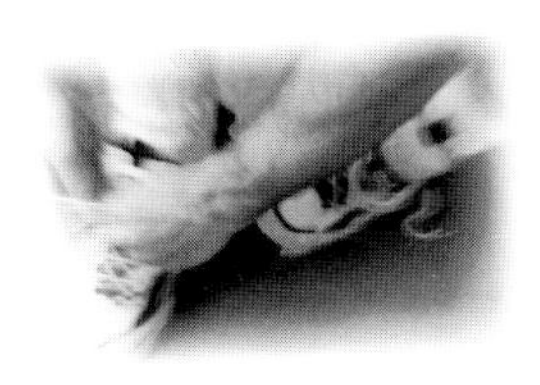

Pressing On to the Prize

But the worries of this life, the deceitfulness of wealth
and the desires for other things come in
and choke the word, making it unfruitful.

week three

Mark 4:19

Pressing On to the Prize

week three

Mark 4:19

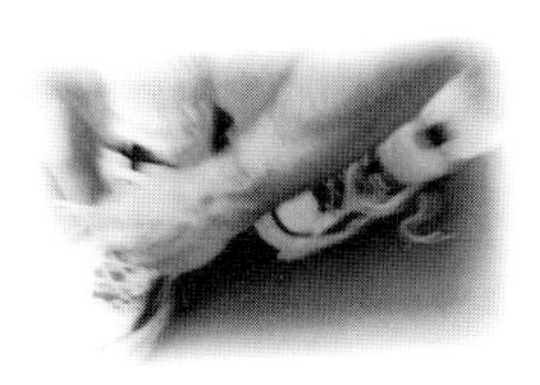

Pressing On to the Prize

And over all these virtues put on love,
which binds them all together in perfect unity.

week four

Colossians 3:14

Pressing On to the Prize

week four

Colossians 3:14

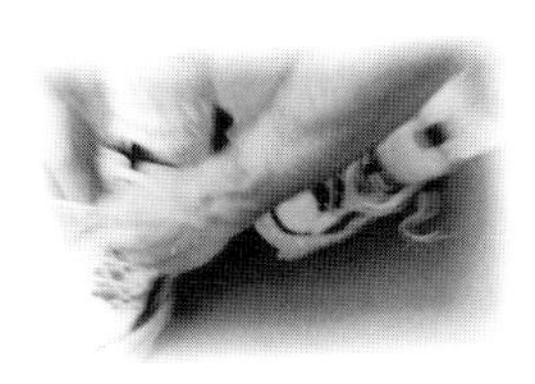

Pressing On to the Prize

But you, man of God, flee from all this,
and pursue righteousness, godliness, faith, love,
endurance and gentleness.

week five

1 Timothy 6:11

PRESSING ON TO THE PRIZE

week five

1 TIMOTHY 6:11

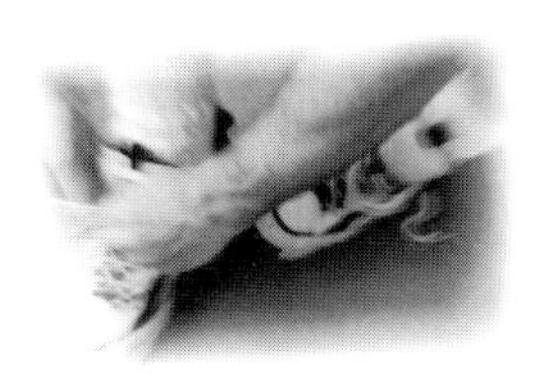

PRESSING ON TO THE PRIZE

Do you not know that in a race all the runners run,
but only one gets the prize?
Run in such a way as to get the prize.

week six

1 CORINTHIANS 9:24

Pressing On to the Prize

week six

1 Corinthians 9:24

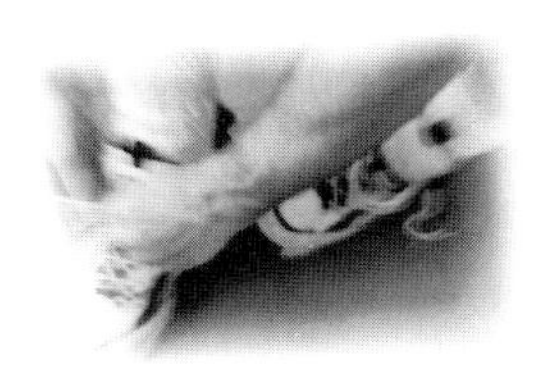

Pressing On to the Prize

And when the Chief Shepherd appears,
you will receive the crown of glory
that will never fade away.

week seven

1 Peter 5:4

PRESSING ON TO THE PRIZE

week seven

1 PETER 5:4

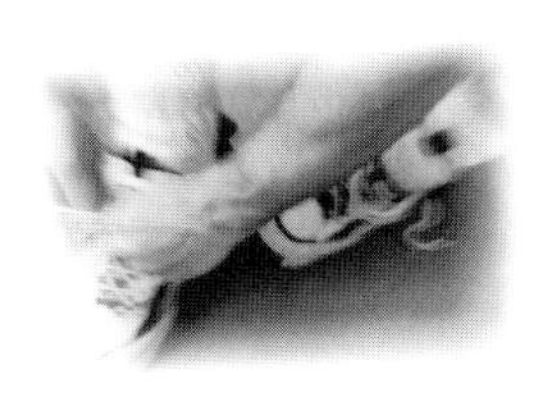

Pressing On to the Prize

Therefore, since we are surrounded by such a great cloud of witnesses, let us throw off everything that hinders and the sin that so easily entangles, and let us run with perseverance the race marked out for us.

week eight

Hebrews 12:1

Pressing On to the Prize

week eight

Hebrews 12:1

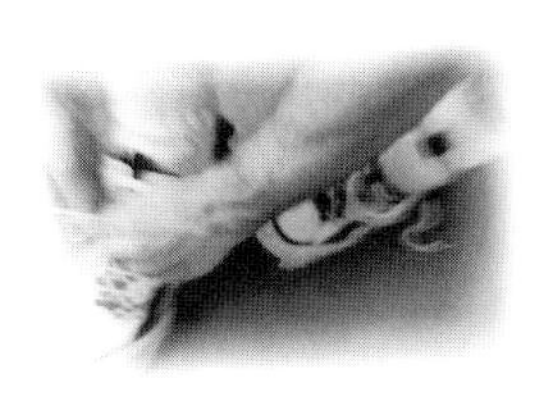

Pressing On to the Prize

Let us fix our eyes on Jesus, the author and perfecter of our faith, who for the joy set before him endured the cross, scorning its shame, and sat down at the right hand of the throne of God.

week nine

Hebrews 12:2

Pressing On to the Prize

week nine

Hebrews 12:2

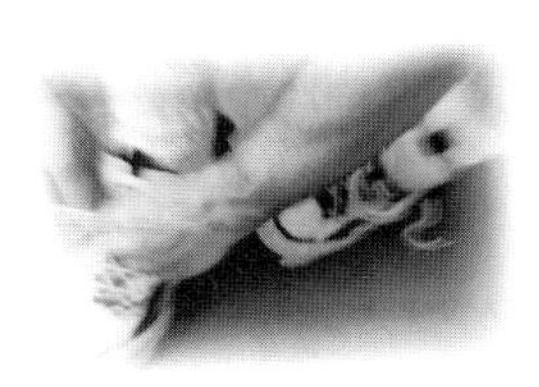

Pressing On to the Prize

See to it that no one misses the grace of God and that no bitter root grows up to cause trouble and defile many.

week ten

Hebrews 12:15

Pressing On to the Prize

week ten

Hebrews 12:15

PATHWAY TO SUCCESS

Where there is no revelation,
the people cast off restraint.

week one

PROVERBS 29:18

Pathway to Success

week one

Proverbs 29:18

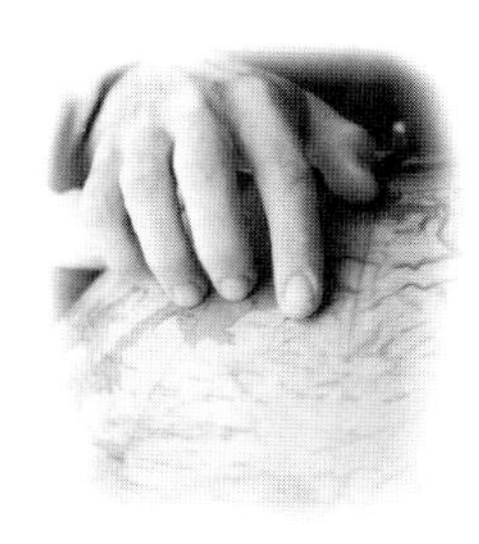

Pathway to Success

May he give you the desire of your heart
and make all your plans succeed.

week two

Psalm 20:4

Pathway to Success

week two

Psalm 20:4

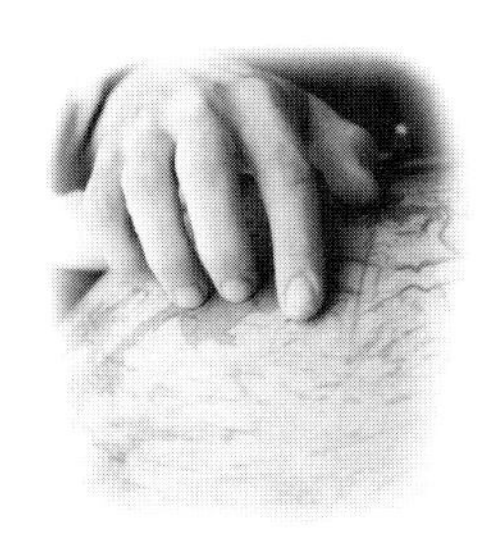

Pathway to Success

Love the Lord your God with all your heart and with all your soul and with all your strength.

week three

Deuteronomy 6:5

Pathway to Success

week three

Deuteronomy 6:5

Pathway to Success

Put on the full armor of God so that you can take your stand against the devil's schemes.

week four

Ephesians 6:11

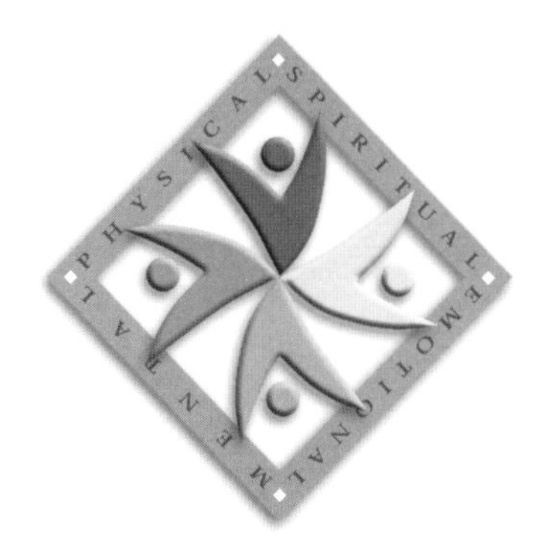

Pathway to Success

week four

Ephesians 6:11

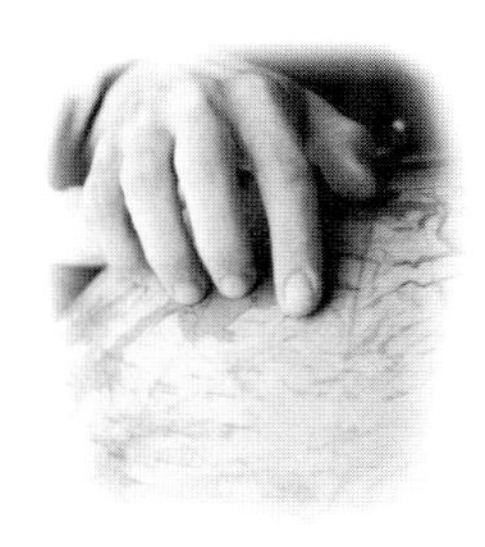

PATHWAY TO SUCCESS

His divine power has given us everything we need for life and godliness through our knowledge of him who called us by his own glory and goodness.

week five

2 PETER 1:3

Pathway to Success

week five

2 Peter 1:3

Pathway to Success

Search me, O God, and know my heart;
test me and know my anxious thoughts.
See if there is any offensive way in me,
and lead me in the way everlasting.

week six

Psalm 139:23,24

Pathway to Success

week six

Psalm 139:23,24

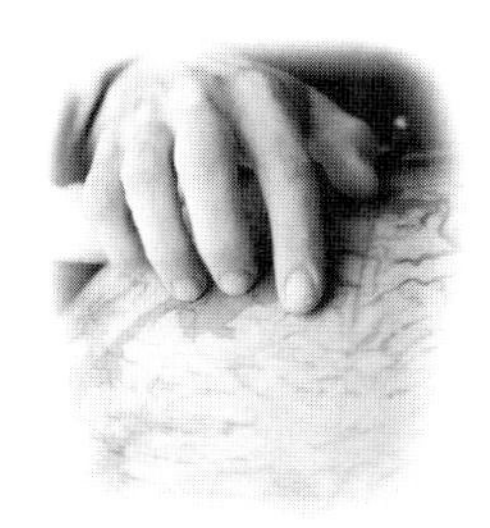

Pathway to Success

Everyone born of God overcomes the world.
This is the victory that has overcome the world,
even our faith. Who is it that overcomes the world?
Only he who believes that Jesus is the Son of God.

week seven

1 John 5:4,5

Pathway to Success

week seven

1 John 5:4,5

Pathway to Success

Whether you turn to the right or to the left,
your ears will hear a voice behind you,
saying, "This is the way; walk in it."

week eight

Isaiah 30:21

Pathway to Success

week eight

Isaiah 30:21

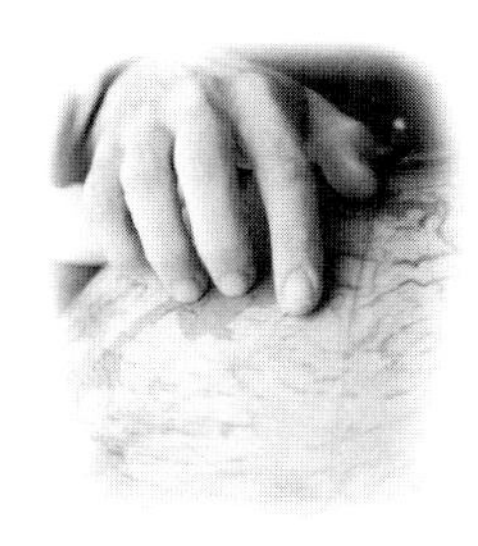

Pathway to Success

Guard the good deposit that was entrusted to you—
guard it with the help of the Holy Spirit who lives in us.

week nine

2 Timothy 1:14

Pathway to Success

week nine

2 Timothy 1:14

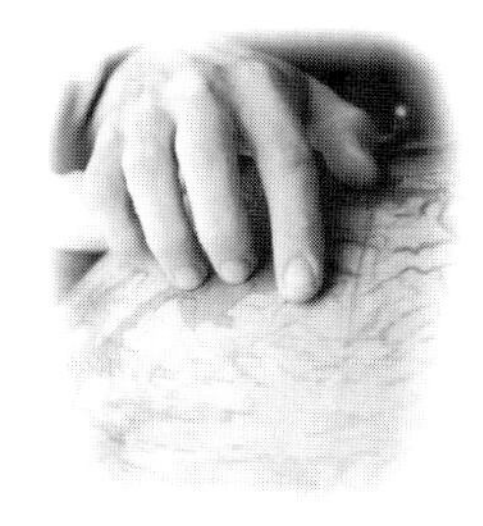

Pathway to Success

You are a chosen people, a royal priesthood,
a holy nation, a people belonging to God,
that you may declare the praises of him who called
you out of darkness into his wonderful light.

week ten

1 Peter 2:9

Pathway to Success

week ten

1 Peter 2:9

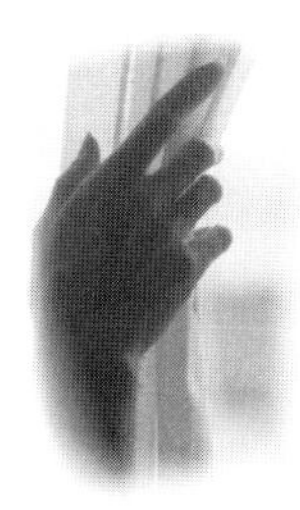

Living the Legacy

He chose us in him before the creation of the world to be holy and blameless in his sight.

week one

Ephesians 1:4

LIVING THE LEGACY

week one

EPHESIANS 1:4

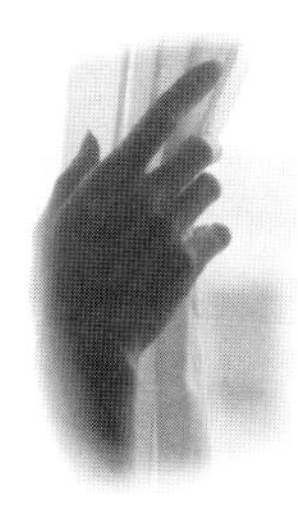

LIVING THE LEGACY

By grace you have been saved, through faith—
and this not from yourselves, it is the gift of God—
not by works, so that no one can boast.

week two

EPHESIANS 2:8,9

LIVING THE LEGACY

week two

EPHESIANS 2:8,9

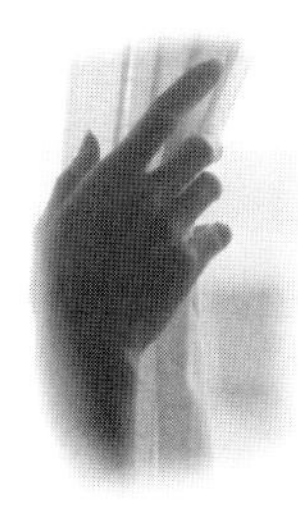

Living the Legacy

He himself is our peace, who has made the two one and has destroyed the barrier, the dividing wall of hostility, by abolishing in his flesh the law with its commandments and regulations.

week three

Ephesians 2:14,15

Living the Legacy

week three

Ephesians 2:14,15

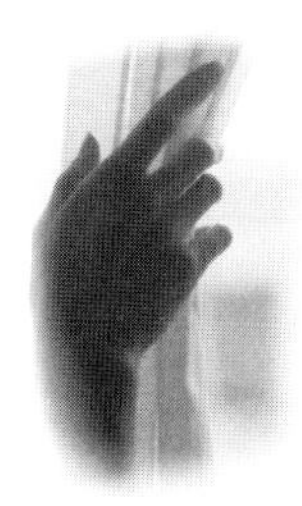

Living the Legacy

Know this love that surpasses knowledge—
that you may be filled to the measure
of all the fullness of God.

week four

Ephesians 3:19

LIVING THE LEGACY

week four

EPHESIANS 3:19

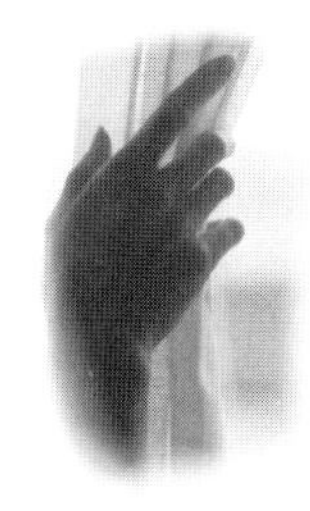

Living the Legacy

You were taught, with regard to your former way of life, to put off your old self, . . . and to put on the new self, created to be like God in true righteousness and holiness.

week five

Ephesians 4:22-24

LIVING THE LEGACY

week five

EPHESIANS 4:22-24

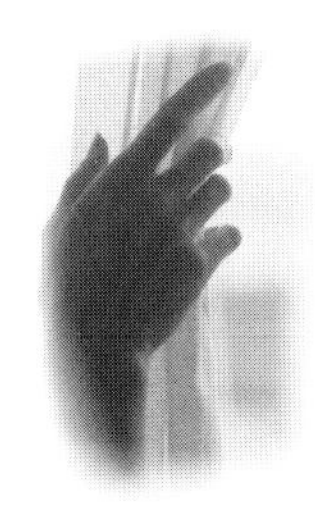

Living the Legacy

Live a life of love, just as Christ loved us and gave himself up for us as a fragrant offering and sacrifice to God.

week six

Ephesians 5:2

Living the Legacy

week six

Ephesians 5:2

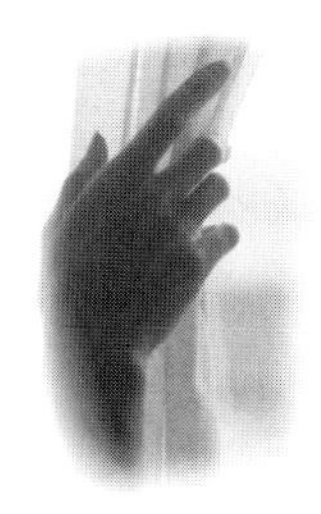

Living the Legacy

You were once darkness, but now you are light in the Lord.
Live as children of light.

week seven

Ephesians 5:8

LIVING THE LEGACY

week seven

EPHESIANS 5:8

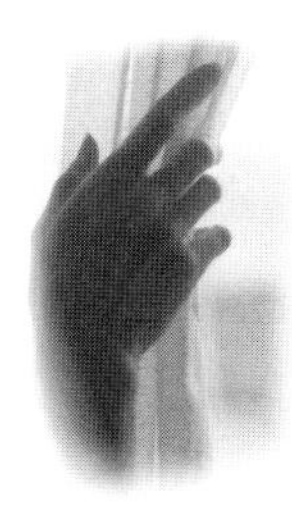

Living the Legacy

Make every effort to keep the unity of the Spirit through the bond of peace.

week eight

Ephesians 4:3

LIVING THE LEGACY

week eight

EPHESIANS 4:3

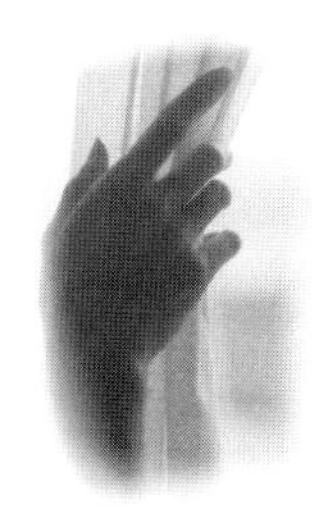

Living the Legacy

Our struggle is not against flesh and blood, but against the rulers, against the authorities, against the powers of this dark world and against the spiritual forces of evil in the heavenly realms.

week nine

Ephesians 6:12

LIVING THE LEGACY

week nine

EPHESIANS 6:12

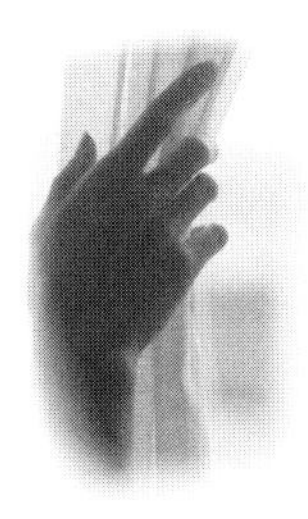

LIVING THE LEGACY

Pray in the Spirit on all occasions with all kinds of prayers and requests.

week ten

EPHESIANS 6:18

LIVING THE LEGACY

week ten

EPHESIANS 6:18

First Place was founded under the providence of God and with the conviction that there is a need for a program that will train the minds, develop the moral character and enrich the spiritual lives of all those who may come within the sphere of its influence.

First Place is dedicated to providing quality information for development of a physical, emotional and spiritual environment leading to a life that honors God in Jesus Christ. As a health-oriented program, First Place stresses the highest excellence and proficiency in instruction with the goal of developing within each participant mastery of all the basics of a lasting healthy lifestyle so that all may achieve their highest potential in body, mind and spirit. The spiritual development of each participant is given high priority so that each may come to the knowledge of Jesus Christ and God's plan and purpose for each life.

First Place offers instruction, encouragement and support to help members experience a more abundant life. Please contact the First Place national office in Houston, Texas, at (800) 727-5223 for information on the following resources:

- ❖ Training Opportunities
- ❖ Conferences/Rallies
- ❖ Workshops
- ❖ Fitness Weeks

Send personal testimonies to:

First Place
7401 Katy Freeway
Houston, TX 77024
Phone:
(800) 727-5223
Website:
www.firstplace.org

THE BIBLE'S WAY TO WEIGHT LOSS

First Place—the Bible-Based Weight-Loss Program Used Successfully by over a Half Million People!

Are you one of the millions of disheartened dieters who've tried one fad diet after another without success? If so, your search for a successful diet is over! First Place is the proven weight-loss program born over 20 years ago in the First Baptist Church of Houston. But First Place does much more than help you take off weight and keep it off. This Bible-based program will transform your life in every way—physically, mentally, spiritually and emotionally. Now's the time to join!

ESSENTIAL FIRST PLACE PROGRAM MATERIALS

Group Leaders need:

- **First Place Group Starter Kit.**
  This kit has everything group leaders need to help others change their lives forever by giving Christ first place!

  Group Starter Kit
  ISBN 08307.28708

Group Members need:

- **First Place Member's Kit.**
  All the material is easy to understand and spells out principles members can easily apply in their daily lives.

  Member's Kit
  ISBN 08307.28694

- **First Place Bible Study**
  Giving Christ First Place
  with Scripture Memory Music CD

  Bible Study
  ISBN 08307.28643

Other Bible studies are available.

FIRST PLACE™ Available at your local Christian bookstore or by calling 1-800-4-GOSPEL.

Join the First Place community at **www.firstplace.org**

Gospel Light

11054